Balsa
Wood
Craft

Balsa Wood Craft

Written and illustrated by
Peter Weiss

Lothrop, Lee & Shepard Co.
New York

Library of Congress Cataloging in Publication Data

Weiss, Peter, 1945–
  Balsa wood craft.

  SUMMARY: Instructions for working with balsa wood
to create doll furniture, toys, party ornaments, and
other items.
  1. Balsa wood craft—Juvenile literature. [1. Balsa
wood craft. 2. Models and modelmaking. 3. Handi-
craft] I. Title.
TT189.W44   745.51   72-1105
ISBN 0-688-40007-8
ISBN 0-688-50007-2 (lib. bdg.)

                    1 2 3 4 5 76 75 74 73 72

Balsa
Wood
Craft

Contents

TOOLS AND MATERIALS   9

WORKING WITH BALSA WOOD   13

TOYS AND GAMES   18

Balancing Parrot   18
Clothespin Zoo   19
King Arthur's Castle   22
Potato Safari   24
Hopping Frog   26
Shooting Gallery   29
Bullseye Box   31

HOLIDAY AND PARTY FUN   33

Party Place Tags   33
Printed Cards and Place Mats   35
Star String   36
Angel Ornament   37
Easter-Bunny Party Favor   39
Turkey Full of Nuts   40
Valentine Plaque   42
Jack-o-Lantern Marble Game   43

DOLL FURNITURE   44

Cradle   44
Doll Tables   45
Armchair and Footstool   47
Rocking Chair   48
Hammock   50

BALSA ART 51

Balsa Printing 51
Stick Sculpture 53
Indian Shield 55
Totem-Pole Wall Hanging 57
African-Lion Mask 59
Funny-Faces Mobile 61

GIFTS 63

Bookmarks 63
Balsa Pendant 64
Photograph Frame 65
Coasters 66
Letter Holder 67
Salt-and-Pepper Server 69
Porch Chimes 71

MODELS 73

Midget Racer 75
Western Buckboard 77
Mississippi Steamboat 80
Pirate Ship 83

SCHOOL PROJECTS 86

Natural Resources Map 86
Animals Around the World 88
Other Ways of Life 90
Famous Buildings 94

INDEX 95

Tools and Materials

BALSA WOOD—Balsa is a lightweight and amazingly soft wood, so soft that it can be cut with a knife. You can buy it in most hobby shops and in some toy stores. Look up "Hobbies" in the *Yellow Pages* and call the stores nearest you to find out if they sell it. Balsa wood comes in many different sizes and shapes, from thin strips and sheets to solid blocks. Before starting a project, read the list of materials needed to make sure you have enough wood of the right thickness, width, and length.

When you buy balsa wood it's a good idea to look over the different pieces in the store and pick the ones that are softest. The softest pieces have an even, light color, with no dark or grayish streaks. They also have wider spaces between the lines marking the grain of the wood. These especially soft pieces are the easiest to cut.

CUTTING TOOLS—The best way to cut balsa wood is with an x-acto knife. It costs about sixty-five cents in a hobby shop or hardware store. It is possible to cut balsa with scissors, a sharp pocketknife, or a single-

x-acto knife
with regular blade

x-acto knife
with number-17
chisel-type blade

edged razor blade, but an x-acto knife is really the easiest and safest tool to use.

Hobby shops sell a variety of replacement blades for x-acto knives. The usual price is about sixty-five cents for a package of five blades. For cutting curved shapes and making holes in balsa wood, it is worth the extra expense to buy a package of number-17 x-acto blades.

CUTTING BOARD—To protect your table or desk, you need a wide wooden board, a piece of masonite or plywood, or just an old magazine.

GLUE—Use a fast-drying white glue, such as Elmer's or Sobo, which you can get in a stationery store or five-and-ten.

PAINT AND BRUSHES—Acrylic paints are best. They dry fast, give bright, shiny colors, and can be washed off your hands with soap and water. If you don't have acrylics, other kinds of paint will do almost as well.

For use with paints that mix with water, like poster paint, tempera paint, or acrylic paint, you need to buy a jar of acrylic medium. This is a white liquid that dries to a shiny, transparent finish.

With non-water paints, like household

enamel, oil colors, or model-airplane enamel, you'll need turpentine to clean your brushes. You'll also need clear shellac to coat the finished projects, and denatured alcohol to clean the brushes used for the shellac.

Whatever kind of paint you use, you'll need three or four different brushes: a tiny one for details, one with bristles about an inch across for large objects, and one or two in-between sizes. Shop around for both paint and brushes—they're very expensive in some stores and cheap in others. Look in five-and-tens, department stores, hobby shops, or art-supply stores.

SCHOOL SUPPLIES—The following items can all be bought in a five-and-ten, stationery store, or office-supply store: tracing paper, carbon paper, construction paper, ruler, compass, and paper fasteners.

Read the list of materials to see what supplies you need for each project.

HARDWARE SUPPLIES—Sandpaper, washers, hook eyes, corks, string, wire, and wooden dowel rods are all available in hardware stores.

SCRAPS, BOXES, ODDS AND ENDS—To make some projects you need scraps of paper, cloth, felt, or wool, or sections cut from mesh produce bags. Other projects call for the use of clothespins, oatmeal boxes, cardboard from shoeboxes or grocery cartons, pins, needles, thread, or spools. Look around the house or ask your parents to help you locate whatever you need. Get their permission before using any household goods in a balsa-wood project.

Working With Balsa Wood

PREPARE A WORK AREA—Clear the top of a table or desk and spread out a newspaper to catch shavings and drops of paint. Put a cutting board or old magazine on top of the newspaper.

STARTING A PROJECT—Read the instructions to make sure you understand what to do. Assemble all the tools and materials needed. Follow the directions step by step.

MEASURING AND MARKING—Use a ruler or yardstick and mark the wood lightly with a soft, dark pencil, sharpened to a good point. Measure the length needed and mark the wood at both ends. Use the ruler to draw a line across the wood connecting the two pencil marks. If you use a compass to draw circles, be sure the pencil in it is a soft one.

TRACING—Hold a sheet of tracing paper on top of the pattern to be traced. Go over all the lines and details with a soft pencil. Use a ruler to trace straight lines.

Transfer the pattern to balsa wood with carbon paper. A whole sheet of carbon paper is awkward to work with, so cut a piece the same size as the piece of balsa. Lay the carbon paper on the wood with the shiny side down. Cover it with the tracing paper, making sure that the pattern is lined up correctly and not sticking out over the edge of the wood. If it's a complicated pattern, you might want to hold the two sheets of paper in place with pins or thumbtacks. Use a ball-point pen to go over the tracing again. Moderate pressure on the pen is enough to transfer the pattern to the wood.

CUTTING BALSA WOOD—Draw the line to be cut right on the wood. Hold the wood steady with one hand while cutting with the other hand. The cutting motion should be in a direction away from the hand holding the wood.

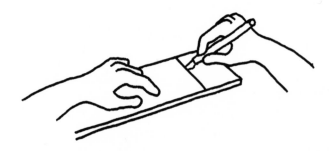

To cut a thick piece of wood, especially if you're cutting across the grain, you may have to go over the line two or three times. Making two or three light cuts is a lot easier than trying to cut all the way through in one stroke. Always use a sharp blade. Replace your x-acto blade with a new one if it seems to be getting dull or rusty.

The best way to cut a curved shape from thick wood is with a number-17 chisel-type x-acto blade. Put the blade on the line and push gently straight down until it goes through the wood. Make a series of small cuts all along the line until the shape is completely cut out. Smooth the cut edge with sandpaper.

Some of the patterns in this book have small black triangles on them, marking spots where holes should be drilled. If you don't have a hand drill in the house, you can use a number-17 x-acto blade to cut out the holes. Just cut straight down into the wood on each side of the triangle.

SANDING—Before painting or gluing, smooth out rough edges with fine sandpaper. The only time to use rough or medium sandpaper is when you want to take off a lot of wood. When you're making something out of a solid block of balsa, you can use rough sandpaper to shape the block the way you want it.

USING GLUE—Spread an even coat of glue on both surfaces to be joined and press them together firmly. Wipe off excess glue with a tissue. Hold the two pieces together for a few minutes until the glue begins to set. Wait at least half an hour before painting.

PAINTING—Balsa wood is so soft and porous that paint sinks right into it instead of staying on the surface. To get a finished product with nice bright colors, you have to start by coating the surface with a primer. If you intend to use paints that mix with water, cover the wood with a primer coat of acrylic medium. Before painting with oil paints, cover the wood with a coat of shellac. Don't put on any paint until the primer coat is dry.

Use paper cups, small jars, or jar lids for mixing different-colored paints together. Put in just a little paint at a time until you get the color you want. It's fun to create your own colors, so don't be afraid to experiment. Mix only paints of the same type—never mix oil and water paints together.

Let each color dry before painting on

the next one. Acrylic paint dries to a strong, waterproof finish, but tempera and poster paints need a final coat of acrylic medium to protect the colors from chipping or rubbing off. Cover oil paints with a final coat of clear shellac.

Hardened paint can ruin your brushes, so wash them as soon as you're done painting. Use either soap and water, turpentine, or denatured alcohol, depending on the kind of paint you used.

CLEANING UP—When you finish a project, fold up and throw away paint-stained newspapers. Pick up wood shavings from the floor. Close glue and paint containers tightly, and put your knife away in a small box or some other safe place. Save any good-sized scraps of balsa wood, because you might want to use them for another project.

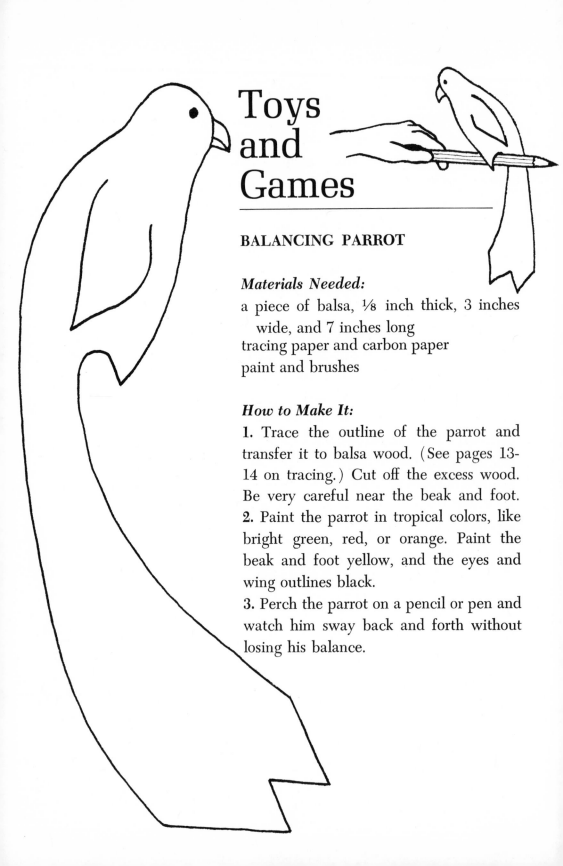

Toys and Games

BALANCING PARROT

Materials Needed:
a piece of balsa, ⅛ inch thick, 3 inches
  wide, and 7 inches long
tracing paper and carbon paper
paint and brushes

How to Make It:
1. Trace the outline of the parrot and
transfer it to balsa wood. (See pages 13-
14 on tracing.) Cut off the excess wood.
Be very careful near the beak and foot.
2. Paint the parrot in tropical colors, like
bright green, red, or orange. Paint the
beak and foot yellow, and the eyes and
wing outlines black.
3. Perch the parrot on a pencil or pen and
watch him sway back and forth without
losing his balance.

CLOTHESPIN ZOO

The three animals shown here are just
the beginning of a zoo. To get ideas for
other animals to make, try looking through
magazines and nature books, or an encyclopedia. It's easier than you might
think to draw a picture of an animal when
you don't have to draw the legs. Remember, also, to leave out tails, horns, or long
thin ears. Make these parts separately, out
of paper. Practice drawing the animal on
paper until you're satisfied; then trace it
and transfer it to balsa wood.

Materials Needed:

wooden spring-type clothespins (two
   clothespins for each animal
a sheet of balsa wood, ⅟₁₆ inch thick, and
   4 inches wide (allow about 7 inches in
   length for each animal you plan to
   make)
tracing paper, carbon paper, and scraps of
   construction paper.
glue, paint, and brushes

How to Make It:
1. Trace an animal on page 20 or 21 and
transfer it to balsa wood. Cut out the
animal shape and clip on clothespins to
make legs. Trace and transfer to con-

struction paper the pattern for the tail. Cut the tail out and glue it onto the animal.

2. Paint the animal, including the clothespin legs. The giraffe might be yellow with brown spots. The camel and lion might be tan or light brown, with the lion's mane a darker color than his body. You can always paint over a color you don't like, so don't be afraid to experiment with colors. Paint the eyes, ears, nostrils, and mouth last, using a thin brush and black paint.

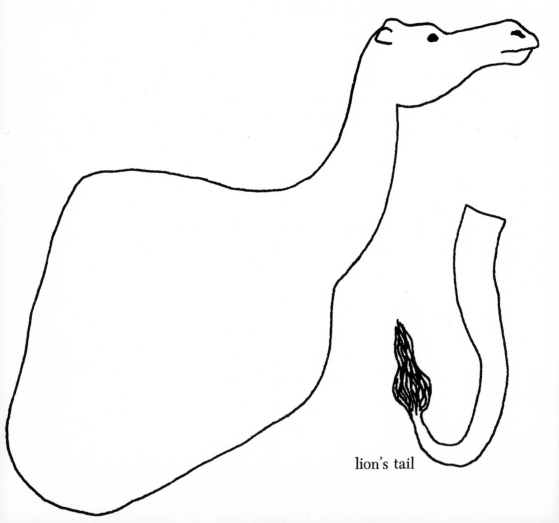

lion's tail

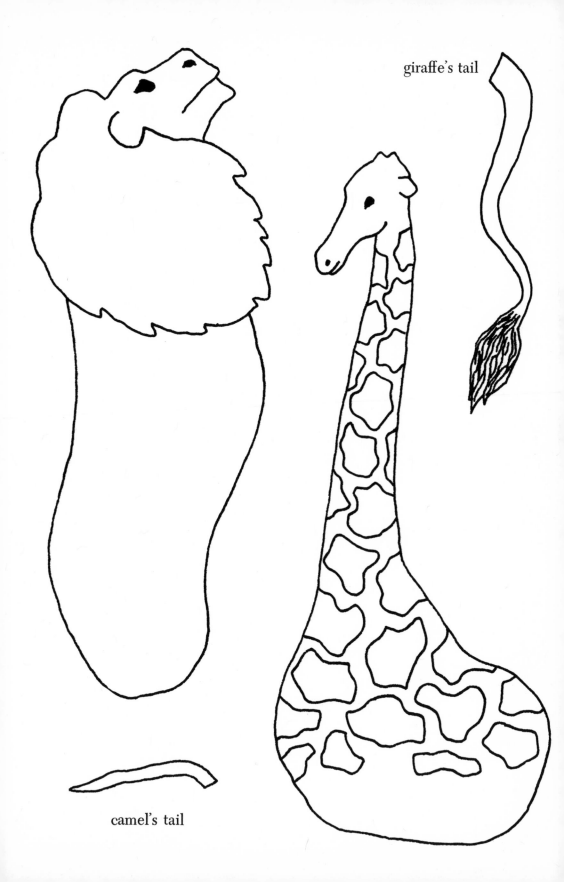

giraffe's tail

camel's tail

KING ARTHUR'S CASTLE

Materials Needed:
four round oatmeal or cornmeal boxes
an 18 inch square of thick cardboard
two sheets of balsa, ⅛ inch thick, 3 inches
    wide, and at least 36 inches long
glue, paint, and brushes

How to Make It:
1. Cut four 10 inch balsa sections and glue them together in a square to make the walls of the castle.
2. Remove the tops from the oatmeal boxes. Cut a piece exactly 3 inches long from each box, as shown in the illustration. Turn the boxes upside down, fit them into position at the four corners of the castle, and glue them in place. Then glue the whole castle to the middle of the cardboard square.
3. Cut the rest of the balsa wood into pieces ½ inch wide and 1 inch long. Glue these pieces along the front of each wall, separated by small open spaces. Half of each piece should stick up above the top of the wall. Glue pieces of balsa around the tops of the oatmeal-box towers in the same way.
4. Paint the cardboard base green. Paint the castle light gray. Use a thin brush to make little squares and rectangles in black,

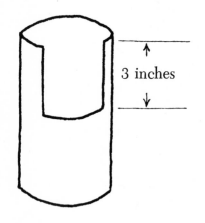

3 inches

brown, and tan, so that the castle seems to
be made of stone. In the middle of one
wall, paint a round-topped closed draw-
bridge, with a stone arch around it. Paint
a blue moat on the base, around the outside walls of the castle.

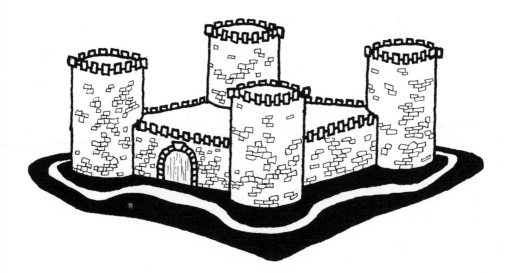

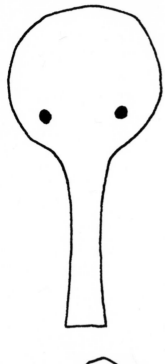

POTATO SAFARI

Materials Needed:
a piece of balsa, ¼ inch thick, 3 inches
    wide, and 6 inches long
four corks, 1¼ inches long (available in
    hardware stores)
a large round potato
four thin, flat-headed nails, 2 inches long
four straight pins, two toothpicks, and a
    scrap from a brown paper bag
glue, paint, brushes, and scissors

How to Make It:
1. Trace and transfer to balsa wood the
elephant head and Indian Maharaja patterns. Cut the patterns out. Use a small
frozen-juice can or a baby-food jar to
trace a circle on the remaining balsa wood.
Cut the circle out. Trace and transfer to
brown paper the elephant-ear pattern, and
cut it out with scissors.

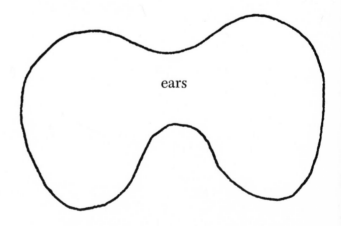

ears

2. Press the point of a nail into the wide end of a cork, right in the center. Carefully push the nail all the way through the cork; then do the same thing with the other corks and nails. Stick the nails into the potato, so that the corks make the four legs of the elephant.

3. Glue the elephant head onto the paper-ear pattern. Glue the Maharaja, in a sitting position, onto the balsa circle.

4. Paint the balsa circle bright red. Paint the Maharaja flesh color all over. Then paint his robe white, his turban blue, and his eyes and beard black. Paint the elephant's eyes black. Stick two pins through the elephant's eyes to attach the head and ears to the potato body. Use the other two pins to hold the balsa circle on the elephant's back. Stick a toothpick into the potato on each side of the trunk to make the tusks.

HOPPING FROG

Materials Needed:
a balsa sheet, ⅛ inch thick, 4 inches wide,
　　and 30 inches long
four round-headed paper fasteners, 1 inch
　　long
eight small metal washers
tracing paper and carbon paper
glue, paint, and brushes

A

D

How to Make It:

1. Trace the patterns and transfer them to balsa wood. Carefully cut out the balsa shapes and mark the correct letter on the back of each one. Cut a small hole at each black triangle.

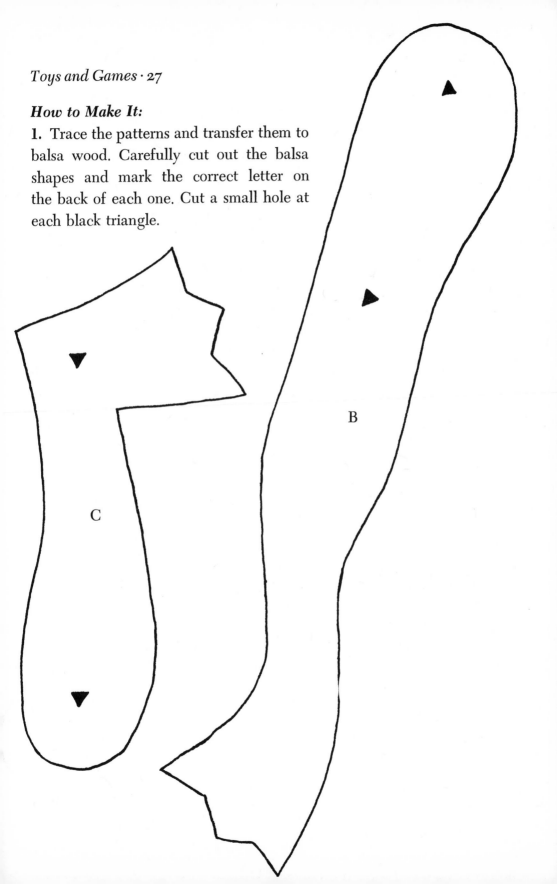

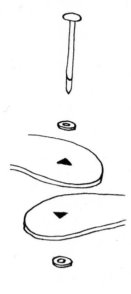

2. Paint the parts light green. (On the front and edges only, not on the back.) Paint dark green spots on the legs and near the right edge of the body. Don't paint spots on the face, belly or feet. Paint on round white eyes. With black paint add the smiling mouth and the pupils of the eyes.

3. Study the diagram showing how to fasten the parts together. Each paper fastener should go through a washer, then through the two pieces of wood, and then through another washer. Following this sequence, fasten parts A and B together through the hole in the middle of each, with A on top of B.

Fasten part A on top of part D, through the holes in the knees.

Fasten part C on top of part B, through the holes in the knees.

Finally, fasten the feet together, with C on top of D.

4. Move the feet like a pair of scissors, and the frog will hop up and down.

SHOOTING GALLERY

Materials Needed:
a sheet of balsa wood, ¼ inch thick, 4
   inches wide, and 18 inches long
tracing paper and carbon paper
large rubber bands
glue, paint, and brushes

How to Make It:
1. Cut a piece 7 inches long from the sheet
of balsa wood. Trace the outline of the gun
and transfer it to the piece of balsa wood.
Cut the gun out.

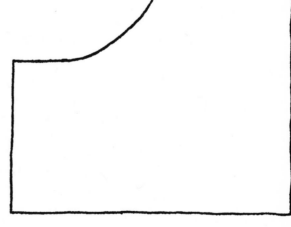

2. Cut a 1 inch section from the remaining balsa wood. Then cut this section into four 1 inch squares. You will be left with a sheet of balsa wood 4 inches wide and 10 inches long. Trace the outline of the bowling pin and transfer it four times to the balsa wood. Cut out the four bowling pins.

3. Glue each bowling pin, standing up, on top of a 1 inch square of balsa wood. Paint the gun and the bowling pins whatever colors you like.

How to Play the Game:

Line the pins up on the floor, in a corner. Shoot from across the room. Hook a rubber band into the notch in the end of the gun barrel. Pull the rubber band back along the top of the gun, aim, and shoot.

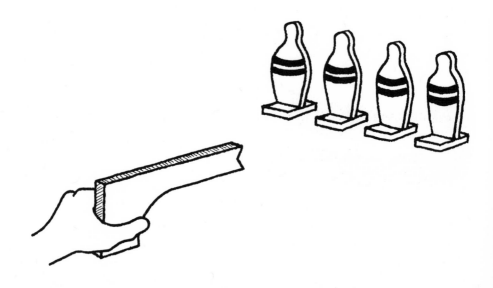

BULLSEYE BOX

Materials Needed:
a sheet of balsa, ¼ inch thick, 3 inches
    wide, and 19 inches long
a strip of balsa, ½ inch thick, ½ inch
    wide, and 10 inches long
one quarter and five pennies
glue, paint, and brushes

How to Make It:
1. Measure and cut two 3½ inch sections
from the sheet of balsa. Cut the rest
of the sheet into four 3 inch squares.
2. Glue three of the 3 inch squares together, as shown in the illustration, forming the bottom and two opposite sides of
a box. Glue the 3½ inch sections in
place to make the other two sides of the
box. The shorter ends of these two sections
should be at the corners of the box, with
the longer edges at the top and bottom.
3. Cut the 10 inch strip of balsa into four
equal parts, each exactly 2½ inches long.
Glue these, standing up, inside the four
corners of the box. When the glue is dry,
paint the box white, inside and out.
4. Put the quarter in the center of the remaining 3 inch square and trace a circle
around it with a pencil. Cut out the circle.
(See page 14 on cutting curved shapes.)

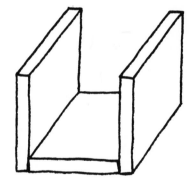

This square with the hole in it is the box top, and it should fit just inside the box, resting on the four posts in the corners. If it's a little too big, sandpaper the edges until it fits snugly. DO NOT GLUE IT DOWN. Paint the top white, and then paint a bullseye design in bright colors around the hole.

How to Play the Game:
Put the bullseye box on the floor. Stand over it without bending your knees, and see if you can drop five pennies in a row through the hole.

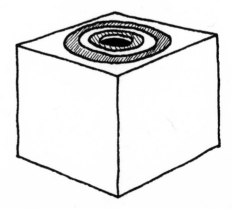

Holiday and Party Fun

PARTY PLACE TAGS

Materials Needed:

sheets of balsa, ⅛ inch thick and 4 inches
  wide (allow 3 inches in length for each
  place tag you plan to make)
tracing paper and carbon paper
glue, paint, and brushes

How to Make It:

1. Cut the balsa wood into sections 3
inches long. Cut each section into two
pieces—one 3 inches square, and the other
1 inch wide and 3 inches long. Trace one
of the patterns or make up one of your
own, and transfer it to each of the 3 inch
squares. Cut out the balsa shapes.

2. Glue each balsa cutout, standing up, at
one end of a 1 by 3 inch base. Paint the
place tags in appropriate colors—a Christmas tree green, a pumpkin orange with

black features, and so on. Use contrasting colors to paint the name of a party guest on the base of each place tag.

PRINTED CARDS AND PLACE MATS

You can use Balsa Printing (see page 51) to make your own original place mats or holiday greeting cards.

Materials Needed:

balsa printing materials
large, solid-colored paper towels
envelopes and construction paper

How to Make It:
GREETING CARDS
1. Cut the paper into rectangles a little less than twice the size of your envelopes. Fold the rectangles in half, making cards that will fit in the envelopes.
2. Print a design on the front of each card. Practice on scrap paper first, to see how much paint to use. Inside each card write a note to the person you're sending it to.

PLACE MATS
1. Print the design you want on the paper towels.
2. Wait for the paint to dry, and then set them out on the table.

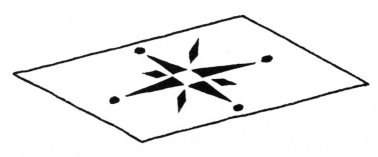

STAR STRING

Materials Needed:
a sheet of balsa, ⅛ inch thick, 4 inches
    wide, and about 3 feet long
silver or gold glitter (available in hobby
    shops and five-and-ten-cent stores)
a needle and thread
glue, paint, and brushes

How to Make It:
1. Cut the balsa sheet into 2 inch squares.
Draw a star on each square. Carefully cut
the stars out. Paint some of the stars white,
some red, and some green.
2. Lay the stars out flat on an open newspaper and put a few drops of glue on
each one. Sprinkle on the glitter and wait
for the glue to dry. Shake off excess glitter
and turn the stars over. Repeat the same
process for the other side.
3. String the stars on a thread by pushing
a needle right through the middle of each
star. Drape the string of stars around the
Christmas tree, or hang it around a doorway or window.

ANGEL ORNAMENT

Materials Needed:

a sheet of balsa, ¼ inch thick and 3 inches wide (you need a piece about 9 inches long for each angel)

one tiny hook eye for each angel

string, glue, paint, and brushes

How to Make It:

1. Trace and transfer to balsa wood the patterns for the angel and the wings. Cut away the excess wood. Screw the hook eye

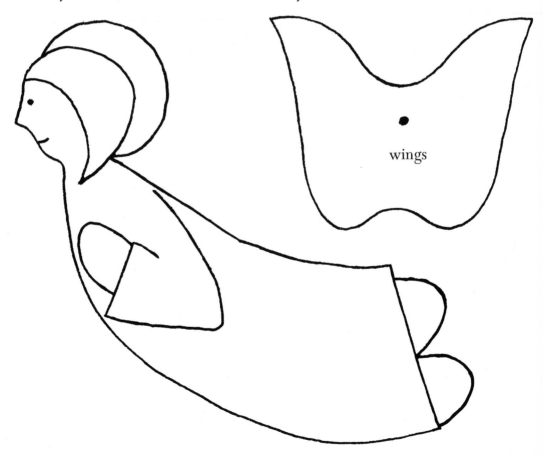

wings

into the dot at the center of the wings.
Unscrew the hook eye, put glue in the hole,
and screw it in again.

2. Glue the wings to the flat edge of the
angel's back. Wait for the glue to dry.
Paint the whole angel white; then paint
the hands, feet, and face a flesh color. The
wings and halo might be pink, yellow,
silver, or gold. The eyes, mouth, hair, and
sleeve outline can be whatever colors you
want.

3. Tie a loop of string to the hook eye
and hang the angel on the Christmas tree.

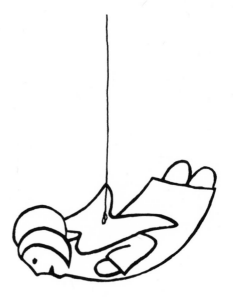

EASTER-BUNNY PARTY FAVOR

These directions tell you how to make one Easter bunny. If you want to make a lot of them you might have to use a whole sheet of ⅛ inch thick balsa wood. The glue and food coloring do not penetrate the egg shell, so the eggs can be eaten when the Easter party is over.

Materials Needed:
some scrap pieces of ⅛ inch thick balsa
an egg
a small piece of fluffy cotton
food coloring
tracing paper and carbon paper
glue, black paint, and a thin brush

rabbit's feet

How to Make It:
1. Put the egg in a pot of cold water. Add several drops of food coloring. Boil the egg for fifteen minutes; then take it out and let it cool.
2. Trace the patterns for the head and feet and transfer them to balsa wood. Cut out both patterns. Paint on the face and the lines on the rabbit's feet. Glue the egg on top of the cut-out feet pattern, with the small end of the egg at the rear. Glue the head to the front of the egg. To finish the bunny, glue the tail to the other end.

TURKEY FULL OF NUTS

Materials Needed:
a sheet of balsa, ¼ inch thick, 4 inches
  wide, and 10 inches long
a round oatmeal or cornmeal box
two thumbtacks
glue, paint, and brushes

How to Make It:
1. Draw a line around the oatmeal box, 2½ inches from the bottom. Cut off the part of the box above the line. The bottom of the box will be the turkey's body.
2. Cut the balsa sheet in half. On one half draw a fan-shaped turkey tail, as shown in the illustration. On the other half, draw the turkey's head and neck. Cut out these two shapes.
3. Glue the tail flat against one side of the oatmeal-box body. Glue the edge of the neck to the opposite side of the body so that the head faces away from the tail. Stick a thumbtack from the inside of the body through the cardboard and into the neck. Do the same thing on the other side, with the thumbtack going through the cardboard and into the tail.
4. Paint the whole turkey a dark color, like brown. Then use a small brush to paint feathers of different colors on the tail.

Paint the beak yellow or orange, and the eyes black. Finish with two coats of acrylic medium or clear shellac.

Fill the turkey with candy, nuts, or dried fruit, and use it as a centerpiece on the Thanksgiving table.

VALENTINE PLAQUE

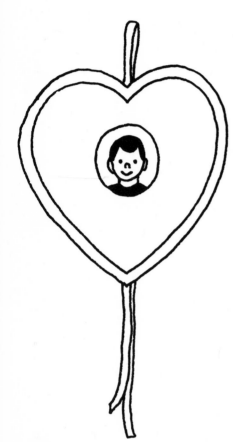

Materials Needed:
a 4 inch square of balsa, ⅛ inch thick
a sheet of white paper
a 2-foot length of red ribbon
a small photograph of yourself
glue, paint, and brushes

How to Make It:
1. Draw a heart, as large as possible, on the square of balsa wood. Cut out the heart and paint one side of it bright red.
2. Cut a circular piece from the photograph, with your face in the center. Glue the circle on the red side of the heart. When the glue is dry, turn the heart over. Double the ribbon and glue it down flat on the back of the heart so that a loop sticks out past the top of the heart and the two long ends hang down past the bottom.
3. Cut a white paper heart slightly larger than the balsa one. Glue the paper heart to the back of the balsa heart. Use the loop in the ribbon to hang the plaque on the wall.

JACK-O-LANTERN MARBLE GAME

Materials Needed:
a sheet of balsa wood, ⅛ inch thick, 4
 inches wide, and 19 inches long
five marbles
glue, paint, and brushes

How to Make It:
1. Cut an 8 inch section of balsa. Draw a
jack-o-lantern on it, as shown, with an
open mouth at the bottom edge. The
mouth should be 2 inches wide and about
1½ inches high. Cut out the mouth open-
ing.
2. Paint the pumpkin orange. Paint the
eyes and nose black, and paint the back-
ground black too. When the paint is dry,
turn the jack-o-lantern face down.
3. Cut two 4 inch squares of balsa. Glue
them, standing on edge, across the back of
the 8 inch section, on both sides of the
mouth. Glue on the remaining piece of
balsa, connecting the two 4 inch squares.

How to Play the Game:
Place the jack-o-lantern on a carpet or
rug. Take turns shooting the marbles from
3 or 4 feet away. The player who gets the
most marbles into the mouth wins the
game.

Doll Furniture

CRADLE

Materials Needed:

a sheet of balsa, ⅛ inch thick, 3 inches wide, and 24 inches long

a compass and a sheet of construction paper

scraps of cloth

glue, paint, and brushes

How to Make It:

1. Cut two 6 inch pieces from the sheet of balsa wood. Glue them together along the long edges so that they form an "L" shape when seen from the ends.

2. Set the two points of the compass exactly 3 inches apart. Draw a circle on the construction paper. Cut out the paper circle and fold it in half. Run a pencil point around the outline of the folded paper to draw two half circles on the remaining balsa wood. Cut out the balsa half circles. They will be rockers for the cradle. Sand the edges smooth, if necessary, and glue the rockers to the ends of the cradle.

3. Paint the cradle and pad the inside with folded scraps of cloth. If you want to decorate the cradle, glue on beads or sequins, or cover the rockers with Con-Tact paper.

DOLL TABLES

Materials Needed:

a sheet of balsa, ⅛ inch thick, 4 inches
  wide, and as long as you want your table
  to be
a strip of balsa, ½ inch thick and ½ inch
  wide (the length depends on the height
  of the table)
glue, paint, and brushes

How to Make It:

COFFEE TABLE

1. Cut a piece of sheet wood the size you
want the tabletop to be. Trim the corners
if you want a round or oval table.
2. To make the legs, cut four 2 inch pieces
from the strip of balsa and glue them to
the top. Use lots of glue.
3. Paint the table.

DINING TABLE

1. The top of a dining table is also made
from a sheet of balsa. The legs are longer,
though, and have to be attached in a
different way. Cut four 5 inch pieces from
the balsa strip. These are the legs.
2. From the rest of the strip cut two pieces
2 inches shorter than the length of the
tabletop. Then cut two pieces 1 inch
shorter than the width of the tabletop.
3. Glue these four pieces so that they lie

flat on the tabletop, forming a hollow rectangle. (See the illustration.)

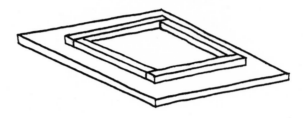

4. Glue the legs, standing up, in the corners of the rectangle. Use plenty of glue.

5. When the glue is completely dry, turn the table right-side up. If it wobbles, figure out which legs are too long and shorten them by gently rubbing with sandpaper or an emery board.

6. Paint the finished table.

ARMCHAIR AND FOOTSTOOL

cut off this part

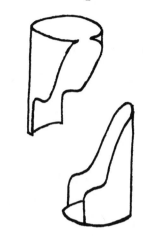

Materials Needed:

a strip of balsa, ½ inch thick, ½ inch wide, and 16 inches long

a sheet of balsa, ¼ inch thick, 4 inches wide, and 7 inches long

a round oatmeal or cornmeal box, regular size

scraps of felt or thick fabric

glue, paint, and brushes

How to Make It:

1. Cut the 16 inch strip into eight pieces, each 2 inches long. These will be the legs for the chair and footstool. Trace around the top of the oatmeal box to draw a circle on the sheet of balsa wood, close to one end. On the rest of the balsa sheet, draw an oval shape 3 inches long and 2 inches wide. Cut out the oval and the circle.

2. Glue four of the legs to the balsa oval to make the footstool. Use plenty of glue. Glue the other four legs to the balsa circle. Cut the body of the chair from the oatmeal box, as shown in the illustration. Glue the body of the chair on top of the balsa circle.

3. Paint the chair and the footstool, but don't put any paint on the top of the stool or the seat of the chair. Cut scraps of felt to the right shapes, or fold up scraps of fabric, and glue them to the seat of the chair and the top of the footstool.

ROCKING CHAIR

Materials Needed:
a sheet of balsa, ⅛ inch thick, 4 inches
    wide, and 24 inches long
tracing paper and carbon paper
glue, paint, and brushes.

How to Make It:
1. Cut the two 2 inch pieces from the balsa
sheet. These will be the seat and the backrest.
2. Trace the chair side and the rocker, and
transfer each pattern twice to the balsa
wood. Cut out the two rockers and the two
chair sides.
3. Get someone to hold the sides in an upright position while you glue the seat and
the backrest in place. If you want, you can
use a few straight pins to hold these pieces
on until the glue dries.
4. Glue a rocker to each side of the chair,
with the top of the rocker on the same level
as the dotted line. Paint the finished chair.

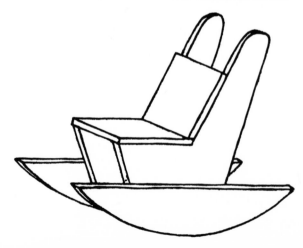

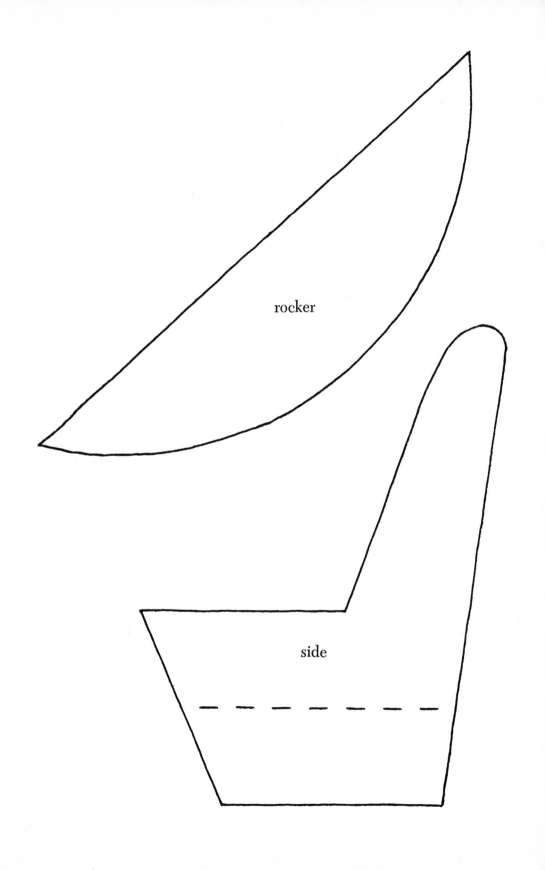

rocker

side

HAMMOCK

Materials Needed:
a sheet of balsa wood, ¼ inch thick, 3
   inches wide, and 23 inches long
six thumbtacks
a piece of mesh, 3 inches wide and 16
   inches long, cut from a bag that oranges,
   onions, or potatoes come in
glue, paint, and brushes

How to Make It:
1. Cut a 3 inch square from one end of
the balsa wood. Draw a line connecting
two opposite corners of the square. Cut
along the line, dividing the square into two
triangles. Cut two 4 inch sections from
the balsa, leaving a piece 12 inches long.
2. Glue the two 4 inch sections upright
across the ends of the 12 inch piece. This
is the frame that will support the hammock. For extra strength, glue a triangle,
standing up, at each angle between the
base and the uprights.
3. Use three thumbtacks to attach one
end of the mesh hammock to the outside
of an upright, close to the top. Use the
rest of the thumbtacks to attach the other
end of the hammock to the outside of the
other upright. If the hammock is stretched
too tight, move the thumbtacks higher. If
it's too loose, move the thumbtacks lower.

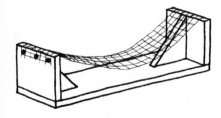

Balsa
Art

BALSA PRINTING

Materials Needed:

a sheet of balsa, ¼ inch thick, 4 inches
   wide, and at least 5 inches long
scraps of ¼ inch thick balsa wood
sheets of paper, white or colored
glue, paint, and brushes

How to Make It:

1. Using the ¼ inch thick sheet of balsa
wood as a base, arrange flat scraps of balsa
to make an abstract design, a face, or a
picture of something—an animal, tree,
house, boat, or anything you like. Cut the
scraps to get whatever shapes you need.
When you're satisfied with the design,
glue the scraps to the base. Wait for the
glue to dry.

2. Paint the raised surface of the design.
You can use two, or even three, different
colors, but it's best to start with a single
color design and work your way up to a
fancier one. While the paint is still wet,
turn the base over and press the design
down on a sheet of paper. Lift the balsa

base straight up from the paper to avoid smearing the printed design. The amount of paint you use will affect the quality of the printing. If the paper shows through the printed areas, you need to use a thicker coat of paint. After one or two tries you'll be able to get it just right.

If you want to make a larger print you might use a piece of wood or thick masonite for a base. The design can be any size you like, but don't make it so big that the paint dries before you have a chance to print it.

STICK SCULPTURE

Materials Needed:
two or three strips of balsa, ⅛ inch thick,
    ¼ inch wide, and at least 3 feet long
scraps of balsa left over from other projects
glue

How to Make It:
1. Cut two 1 foot strips of balsa. Cut the rest of the balsa strips into random lengths from 2 to 7 inches long. Glue a short strip across one end of each 1 foot piece, forming long "T" shapes.
2. Pick out a large flat scrap of balsa to use as a base. Turn the "T" shapes upside down and glue the crossbars to the base, with the long strips sticking straight up in the air. The exact placement of these pieces doesn't make much difference, but they should be at least 2 or 3 inches apart. Use plenty of glue to attach them to the base. Connect the tops of the two uprights with a short balsa strip. This completes the framework for whatever sculpture you want to make.
3. An abstract sculpture can be made by gluing on strips of balsa sticking out in all directions, and adding flat scraps of various shapes.
    You can make a human figure by using

the upright strips as legs and gluing on
scraps to make a body and head. Use short
strips and scraps to make arms, hands, feet,
and a face. Reinforce the legs by gluing on
more short strips.

Other possibilities are a large head or
face, a bird, or an animal. Attach just one
or two pieces at a time; then decide on
the next piece to add while you wait for
the glue to dry. You may have to lay the
sculpture on its side so that a piece will
stay in place while the glue is drying.

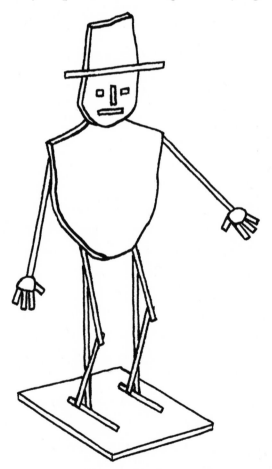

INDIAN SHIELD

Materials Needed:
a sheet of balsa, ¼ inch thick, 4 inches
  wide, and 26 inches long
one tiny hook eye
a compass and a sheet of paper
two or three feathers
string, glue, paint, and brushes

How to Make It:
1. Set the two points of the compass exactly 4 inches apart and draw a circle on a sheet of paper. Cut out the paper circle and fold it in half. Draw two half circles on the balsa wood by tracing the outline of the folded paper. Cut out the two balsa half circles.
2. Cut a 6 inch piece from the remaining balsa wood. On this piece draw the outline of a thunderbird, as shown in the illustration. Cut out the thunderbird.
3. Glue the two half circles together, edge to edge. Glue the thunderbird onto the front of the completed balsa circle. You should still have a piece of balsa wood about 4 inches square. Glue this piece on the back of the balsa circle to provide extra strength. Wait for the glue to dry.
4. Paint the shield white, tan, or some other light color. Paint the thunderbird in

two or three darker colors. When the paint is dry, screw the hook eye into the square on the back of the shield, near the top. Tie the feathers to a piece of string and tie the string to the hook eye, with the feathers hanging at the bottom of the shield. Use another length of string to hang the shield on the wall.

TOTEM-POLE WALL HANGING

Materials Needed:
a sheet of balsa, ¼ inch thick, 4 inches
   wide, and 30 inches long
one tiny hook eye
tracing paper and carbon paper
glue, paint, and brushes

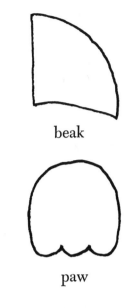

beak

paw

How to Make It:
1. Cut off a 12 inch section of balsa wood
and set it aside. On the rest of the sheet
of wood draw three shapes similar to the
ones shown. Don't worry if they're not
exact copies—the Indians never made two
identical totem poles. Cut away the excess
wood.
2. To make the eagle's wings, cut a 4 inch
long piece of balsa from the 12 inch section
of balsa. Cut this piece in half from corner
to corner, making two triangles. Trace the
paw pattern and transfer it four times to
the remaining balsa wood. Trace the beak
and transfer it to balsa wood too. Cut out
the beak and the four paws. Cut the leftover scraps of balsa to make four round
eyes, two nose shapes, and a square mouth.
3. Glue the beak to the eagle's head. Glue
the four paws to the body of the middle
figure. Glue eyes and a nose to the middle
figure's head. Glue eyes, a nose, and the

square mouth to the bottom figure on the totem pole. Glue a corner of each wing to the back of the eagle, with most of the wing sticking out to the side.

4. Screw the hook eye into the back of the eagle's head. Paint the whole totem pole brown, then paint the features in any combination of blue, red, brown, or white. Hang the totem pole on the wall with a piece of string or wire.

AFRICAN-LION MASK

Materials Needed:
a sheet of balsa, ¼ inch thick, 4 inches
    wide, and 38 inches long
one tiny hook eye
a ball of wool or string in a dark color
glue, paint, and brushes

How to Make It:
1. Cut two 12 inch pieces of balsa wood.
Glue them together edge to edge, to make
one 8 inch wide piece. Round off the
corners to make an egg shape, with one
end a little smaller than the other.
2. Cut a 6 inch piece of balsa wood and
cut off the corners to get a kite shape. Glue
the kite-shaped piece to the front of the
mask in the position shown. Glue on the
two largest cut-off corners to make eyes.
Cut two 4 inch balsa squares and round
off the corners. These two pieces will be
the ears. Glue the ears to the back of the
mask, near the top, sticking out on the
sides.
3. Paint the front of the mask brown or
tan. Paint the eyes yellow. Paint the kite-
shaped piece black, and paint a black
mouth below it. Paint a vertical black line
across each eye.
4. Screw the hook eye into a flat scrap of

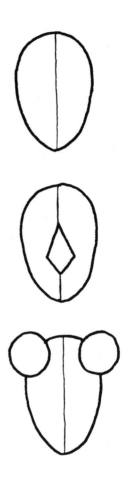

balsa wood and glue the scrap to the back of the mask, halfway between the ears. Make the lion's mane by cutting 4 inch lengths of string or wool and gluing them all around the back edges of the mask. Hang the mask on the wall with a loop of string or wire.

FUNNY-FACES MOBILE

Materials Needed:
scraps of balsa wood left over from other
　　projects
a sheet of balsa, ¼ inch thick, 4 inches
　　wide, and 16 inches long
four tiny hook eyes, the smallest size pos-
　　sible
three ¼ inch dowel rods—one 18 inches
　　long and two 12 inches long
heavy-duty thread, glue, paint, and
　　brushes

How to Make It:
1. Cut the balsa sheet into four 4 inch
sections. Trim the corners to make four
different head shapes—round, pear-shaped,
oblong, or any irregular shapes you like.
Decide which part of each head is the top
and screw a hook eye into the edge of
the wood at that point. Unscrew the hook
eyes, put a drop of glue into each hole,
and screw them in again.
2. The real fun comes when you start
gluing features onto the faces. A long
pointed scrap of balsa can be a nose, sticking out from the face. Another kind of nose
could be made by gluing on a flat balsa
circle or triangle. Use other balsa scraps
to make eyes and mouths. Cut the scraps,

if necessary, to get the shapes you want. You might make one or two animal faces, with big balsa ears, tusks, or long horns. When the glue is completely dry, paint the four faces. When the paint dries, turn the faces over and paint the backs in solid colors.

3. Cut shallow notches near both ends of each dowel rod. Use pieces of thread a few inches long to tie one funny face to each end of the two 12 inch dowels. Put a little glue on the knots to ensure a tight hold. Tie a 6 inch piece of thread to the middle of each 12 inch dowel. To balance the dowels, pick them up, one at a time, by the center threads. Slide the knotted thread back and forth until the dowel hangs in a horizontal position. Then put glue on the knots.

4. Tie the two center threads to the ends of the 18 inch dowel. Put glue on the knots. Tie a 12 inch long piece of thread to the middle of the 18 inch dowel. Use this thread to hold the mobile up in the air. Slide the knot back and forth along the 18 inch dowel until the whole mobile hangs in a balanced position. Put glue on the knot to hold it in place. The mobile can now be hung from a ceiling beam or a high doorway, where nobody will bump his head on it.

Gifts

BOOKMARKS

Materials Needed:
a piece of balsa, $\frac{1}{16}$ inch thick, 3 inches
   wide, and at least 4 inches long
tracing paper and carbon paper
paint and brushes

How to Make It:
1. Trace one of the patterns or make up
one of your own, and transfer it to the
balsa wood. Cut the bookmark out. If you
picked one with a black design, cut out
the black parts.
2. Paint the bookmark a bright color. If
you made one without a cut-out design,
you might decorate it with a painting of a
flower, bird, tree, or anything you like.

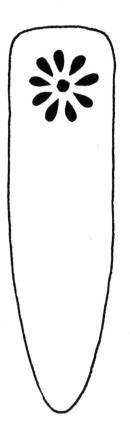

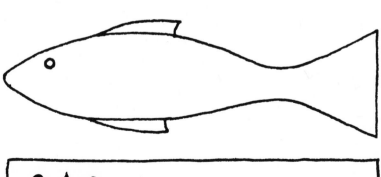

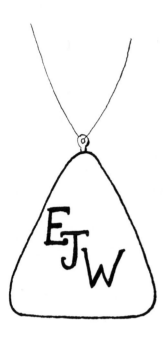

BALSA PENDANT

Materials Needed:
a flat scrap of ¼ inch thick balsa, 2 or 3
    inches wide
one tiny hook eye
glue and nylon thread
paint and brushes, or small beads, sequins,
    or little sea shells

How to Make It:
1. Cut a scrap of balsa wood into whatever shape you want the pendant to be. Decide which part will be the top, and screw a hook eye into the edge of the wood at that point. Unscrew the hook eye, put glue in the hole, and screw it in again.

2. Paint on the pendant a picture of a flower, a happy face, the initials of the person you're making it for, or some other design. If you have beads, sequins, or tiny shells, you might want to glue them on in an attractive pattern instead of painting a design. Whether you used paint or glued-on decorations, cover the finished pendant with two or three coats of acrylic medium. Use clear shellac if you painted with oil paints.

3. Hang the pendant on a loop of nylon thread, making the loop big enough so that it can be slipped over a person's head.

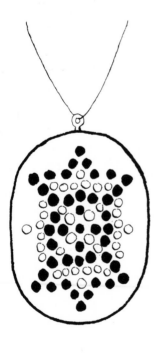

PHOTOGRAPH FRAME

Materials Needed:
a sheet of balsa, ⅛ inch thick, 4 inches
 wide, and 12 inches long
a small photograph of yourself
sandpaper, a ruler, and a compass
glue, paint, and brushes

How to Make It:
1. Cut the balsa sheet into three 4 inch
squares. On one of the squares draw two
straight lines, connecting the opposite
corners. The spot where the lines cross is
the center. Set the metal point and the
pencil point of the compass exactly 1 inch
apart. Put the metal point in the center of
the balsa square and draw a circle. Carefully cut out the circle, leaving a round
hole. Sand the edges of the hole smooth,
and paint the edges with two or three
coats of black paint.
2. Glue the photograph to the square with
the hole in it, so that the face can be seen
through the hole. Glue one of the other
balsa squares to the back of the one with
the photograph. When the glue is dry,
sand the outside edges smooth and flat.
3. Position the squares framing the photograph so that they are standing up on top
of the third square. Glue them in place.
Paint the frame and base.

COASTERS

Materials Needed:
sheets of balsa, ⅟₁₆ inch thick and 4 inches
    wide (allow 8 inches in length for each
    coaster)
sandpaper and a compass
glue, paint, and brushes

How to Make It:

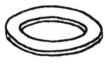
1. Draw a line down the middle of each
balsa sheet, from one end to the other. Be
sure the line is exactly in the middle. Set
the two points of the compass 2 inches
apart. With the metal point of the compass
on the center line, draw circles on the balsa
sheets. Draw two circles for each coaster
you plan to make. Cut out the circles.
2. Count out half of the round balsa pieces
and put them aside to use as bases. On
each of the remaining balsa circles draw
another, smaller circle, 3 inches across.
(Set the two compass points 1½ inches
apart. Put the metal point in the center
hole made when you drew the larger circle.) Carefully cut out the smaller circles,
leaving doughnut-shaped pieces of balsa.
3. Glue each doughnut-shaped piece on
top of a round base. When the glue is dry,
sand the outside edges smooth. Paint the
coasters, and finish with two coats of
acrylic medium or clear shellac.

LETTER HOLDER

Materials Needed:

a balsa sheet, ⅛ inch thick, 4 inches wide,
and 18 inches long

tracing paper, carbon paper, and sandpaper

glue, paint, and brushes

How to Make It:

1. Cut a 6 inch section of balsa to use as a
base. Cut the rest of the sheet of balsa into
three 4 inch squares.

2. Trace the rooster pattern and transfer
it to each of the 4 inch squares. Cut out
the three roosters. Sand the bottom edge
of each rooster's feet to make sure they're
flat and smooth.

3. Glue a rooster, standing up, across each end of the base. Use lots of glue. Glue the third rooster halfway between the first two.

4. Paint the entire letterholder a solid color. Use other colors to paint on tail and wing feathers. Paint the roosters' combs red, and their feet and beaks yellow or orange. Paint the eyes black.

SALT-AND-PEPPER SERVER

Materials Needed:
a balsa sheet, ⅛ inch thick, 4 inches wide,
 and 22 inches long
a balsa strip, ½ inch thick, ½ inch wide,
 and 16 inches long
glue, paint, and brushes

How to Make It:
1. Cut two 8 inch pieces of sheet balsa.
Put one aside to use as a base. Near each
end of the other piece, trace a pencil line
around a salt or pepper shaker. Cut along
the pencil lines to make two holes that the
shakers will fit through.
2. Take the remaining piece of sheet balsa
and round off the corners at one end. Glue
this piece, standing upright, across the
middle of the piece with the holes in it.
3. Cut the balsa strip into four 4 inch
sections. Glue two of them along the bottom of the upright, one on each side. Glue
the other two, side by side, across the middle of the base. Glue the piece with the
holes in it on top of the two strips in the
middle of the base.
4. Paint the salt and pepper server a solid
color. Paint a clown face, a flower, or some
other design on each side of the upright
handle. If you want more decoration, you

could glue on gummed-paper stars, beads, or sequins to make a fancy design around the edges of the two holes. Whatever decoration you use, cover the finished salt and pepper server with two or three protective coats of acrylic medium or clear shellac.

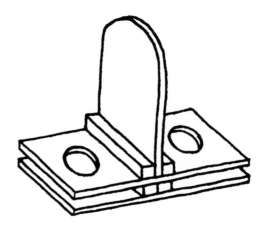

PORCH CHIMES

Materials Needed:
a strip of balsa, ½ inch thick, ½ inch
   wide, and 24 inches long
eight hook eyes
a ¼ inch thick dowel rod, 12 inches long
four large bells, or four clusters of small
   bells (available in hobby shops)
string, glue, paint, and brushes

How to Make It:
1. Cut shallow notches near the ends of
the dowel. Tie the ends of a 24 inch piece
of string to the notches in the dowel. Tie
a 12 inch string to the middle of the
first string, so that you can hang the dowel
rod in a horizontal position.
2. Cut the balsa strip in four 6 inch pieces.
Screw hook eyes into both ends of each
piece. Remove the hook eyes, put a little
glue in each hole, and screw them in again.
Paint the balsa strips with four different
colors, or with stripes or other patterns.
Finish with two coats of acrylic medium.
If you used oil-base paints, finish with two
coats of clear shellac.
3. Use short lengths of string to hang the
balsa strips by their ends from the dowel
rod. Put glue on the knots to keep them
from slipping.

4. Paint the dowel and finish with protective coats as you did the balsa strips.
5. Tie a bell, or a cluster of bells, to the free end of each balsa strip.

Hang the chimes from your porch ceiling or outside a window, where the bells will tinkle cheerfully when the wind blows.

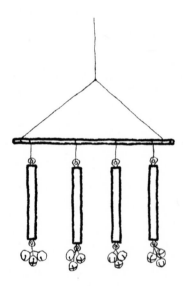

Models

The projects in this section may seem difficult to a beginner, but once you have some experience in working with balsa wood you'll find that they're not too hard at all. Start by making several of the easier projects in other sections and you'll soon develop the skills needed for model-making. To get a really good-looking model you have to work very carefully. All measurements must be exact. Cut edges should be straight and smooth. Glue and paint must be applied evenly and neatly.

If you make the pirate ship or the steamboat you'll need a small saw, like a hacksaw, coping saw, or keyhole saw. Don't try to cut balsa with a full-sized carpenter's saw. It will just rip the soft wood into jagged pieces.

Some of the models can be made to look even more realistic if you add a few extra details before you paint them. You can add a clear cellophane windshield and a wire steering wheel to the racing car. On the steamboat and the pirate ship you can make balsa railings around the edges of the decks. You might also make the little stairways leading from one deck to another. Even without the extra details, you'll be proud to display the models you make on your bookshelf or dresser.

If you're interested in airplanes, toy stores sell balsa glider kits for about 15 cents. These kits come with specially shaped metal weights for the nose of the plane, and sometimes with a plastic pilot and cockpit canopy. When you buy a balsa glider, trace the shapes of all the pieces onto paper before you fit them together. Be sure to trace the narrow cut-out slots in the body of the plane. When the glider is broken in a crash landing, you wont have to throw it away. Just make replacement parts from balsa wood of the right thickness. As long as you have the metal and plastic parts, the plane should last forever, or at least until it gets caught in a tree.

MIDGET RACER

Materials Needed:

a balsa sheet, ¼ inch thick, 3 inches wide,
    and 4 inches long

four straight pins and four small beads

four 1 inch rubber-tired model-airplane
    wheels (available in hobby and model
    shops)

medium and fine sandpaper, glue, paint,
    and brushes

How to Make It:

1. Cut two pieces of balsa 1 inch wide and
4 inches long. Glue one on top of the other
and wait for the glue to dry. Use medium-
grade sandpaper to round the corners at
one end, but remember to leave the bottom flat. At the other end, sand the sides
and top to make the low, narrow front of
the car.

2. Go over the car with fine sandpaper so
that all the surfaces are smooth and
rounded, except for the bottom and the
small flat part at the front. Cut a triangular
notch in the top of the car, 1½ inches
from the back end.

3. Cut two pieces of balsa ¼ inch wide
and 1½ inches long. These are the axles.
Turn the car upside down and glue on the
axles. One should be 1 inch from the front

of the car, and the other should be ½ inch from the back. When the glue dries, paint the whole car a bright color. Paint your favorite number on the hood and on both sides. Finish with acrylic medium or clear shellac.

4. Stick a pin through the hole at the center of one of the wheels, then through one of the beads. Push the pin straight into the end of one axle, as far as it will go. Repeat this step to mount each of the wheels.

WESTERN BUCKBOARD

Materials Needed:

a sheet of balsa, ¼ inch thick, 3 inches
wide, and 36 inches long
two pieces of balsa, ½ inch thick, ½ inch
wide, and 3 inches long
a compass and a piece of fine sandpaper
four 1 inch nails with flat heads
two tiny hook eyes and one tiny safety pin,
as small as possible
glue, paint, and brushes

How to Make It:

1. Set the two points of the compass 1¼
inches apart. Starting at one end of the
balsa sheet, draw four circles. Make them
as close together as possible without overlapping each other. Cut out the circles
and sand the edges smooth. Push a nail
through the center of each circle. Wiggle
the nails around to enlarge the holes until
the balsa circles will spin freely on the
nails.
2. Cut two 7 inch balsa sections. Put one
aside to use as the floor of the buckboard.
From the second section cut two strips 7
inches long and 1 inch wide, and another
strip 7 inches long and ½ inch wide.
3. Cut from the remaining balsa wood two
pieces 2½ inches long and 1 inch wide;

one piece 3 inches long and 1 inch wide;
and one piece 3 inches and ½ inch wide.

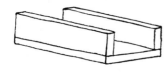

4. Take the two 7 by 1 inch strips and glue
them to the floor of the buckboard, making
the bottom and the long sides of the
wagon body.

5. Glue the two 2½ inch long pieces in
place to make the front and back ends of
the wagon body.

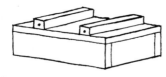

6. The two ½ by ½ inch pieces will be
the axles of the buckboard. Make pencil
marks on the ends of each axle, right in
the center. Push a nail straight into the
wood at each pencil mark; then pull it out
again. Turn the buckboard upside down
and glue the axles to the bottom, 1 inch
from each end.

7. When the glue is dry, screw a hook eye
into one axle, as shown. Screw the other
hook eye into one end of the remaining
7 inch balsa strip. Unscrew both hook
eyes, put glue in the holes, and screw them
in again. Glue the 3 by ½ inch piece
across the 7 inch strip. This crossbar should
be about 2 inches from the end of the strip
with the hook eye in it.

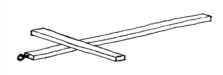

8. You will still have a 3 by 1 inch piece of balsa. Glue this piece to the buckboard to make the seat. Remove the nails from the wheels. Paint all the parts, including the wheels, a solid color. When the paint is dry, use a contrasting color to add spokes and a rim to each of the wheels.

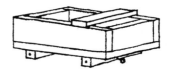

9. Stick a nail through the center of each wheel. If the holes are clogged with dried paint, wiggle the nails around to make the holes bigger. Attach the wheels by pushing the nails straight into the holes on the ends of the axles. Use a safety pin to fasten the two hook eyes together.

MISSISSIPPI STEAMBOAT

Materials Needed:
a piece of balsa, ½ inch thick, 3 inches
 wide, and 20 inches long
a sheet of balsa, ⅛ inch thick, 3 inches
 wide, and 8 inches long
a medium-sized wooden spool, 1¾ inches
 long
a lollipop stick and a wide drinking straw
tracing paper, carbon paper, and sandpaper
a small handsaw
glue, paint, and brushes

How to Make It:
1. Saw off an 8 inch section of ½ inch
thick balsa. Make a blunt point at one end
by sawing off the corners. Round the
pointed end with sandpaper to make the
curved bow (front) of the steamboat. This
piece is the main deck of the boat.
2. Saw the rest of the ½ inch thick balsa
into two 6 inch sections. Cut a 1 inch wide
strip from the side of each section, making
them 2 inches wide. Glue them together,
one on top of the other, to make a single
piece, 1 inch thick and 2 inches wide.
Round off the corners at one end with
sandpaper. Sand the other end and the
sides smooth and flat. Glue this double

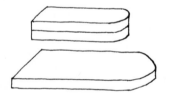

piece down in the middle of the main deck, with the flat end ¾ inch from the flat end of the main deck.

3. From one of the leftover 1 inch wide strips, saw a piece 2 inches long, and a second piece 1 inch long. Sand the edges. Glue the smaller piece on top of the larger piece. This is the pilothouse where the captain stands at the wheel. Glue the pilothouse to the top deck of the steamboat, about 2 inches from the rounded end.

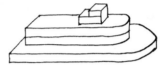

4. Cut two 3 inch sections from the straw. Glue them, standing on end, in front of the pilothouse near the sides of the top deck. Peel off the labels from the ends of the spool. Using ⅛ inch thick balsa, cut eight strips ¼ inch wide and 1¼ inches long. Glue these strips on their edges around the spool. This turns the spool into a paddlewheel.

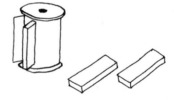

5. Trace the circle and the paddlewheel arm. Transfer each tracing twice to the ⅛ inch thick balsa sheet. Cut out the two circles and the two arms and sand the edges

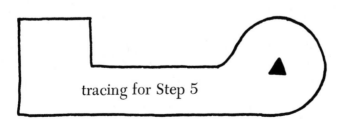

tracing for Step 5

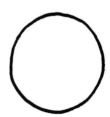

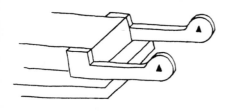

smooth. Cut a hole at each of the black triangles. (See page 15 on cutting holes.)

6. Glue the paddlewheel arms to the rear of the steamboat, as shown. Cut the lollipop stick so that it's just long enough to go through the holes and connect the two arms. The ends of the stick should rest in the holes without sticking out to the sides. Take the stick out. Put the paddlewheel between the arms. Push the stick through the holes in the arms and the spool, so that it holds the paddlewheel in place. Glue the two balsa circles over the holes in the paddlewheel arms.

7. Paint the whole steamboat white. Then paint the deck surfaces tan or brown. Paint the smokestacks and the pilothouse roof black. Use a very thin brush and a bright color, like red, green, or orange, to paint the window and door outlines.

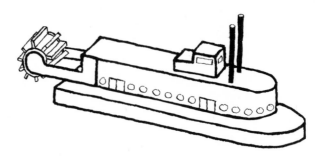

PIRATE SHIP

Materials Needed:

a block of balsa, 2 inches thick, 3 inches
   wide, and 9 inches long

a piece of balsa, ½ inch thick, 3 inches
   wide, and 4 inches long

a dowel rod ⅜ inch thick and 36 inches
   long

a hammer and a 3 inch flat-headed nail

a small handsaw

two pieces of white or tan cloth, 5 inches
   wide and 7 inches long

thread and a paper rectangle, 2 inches
   wide and 4 inches long

glue, paint, and brushes

How to Make It:

1. Glue the ½ inch thick piece, lying flat,
at one end of the block. This will be the
rear deck of the ship. Let the glue dry
completely.

2. At the other end of the block, saw small
pieces from the corners to make the bow.

3. Turn the block on its side. Saw off a
small piece from the bottom of the bow.
Saw off a triangular section from the stern
(back end) to give it a slanted shape.

4. Round off the corners of the bow with
sandpaper, but leave the top and bottom
edges flat. Sand the slanting stern flat and
smooth.

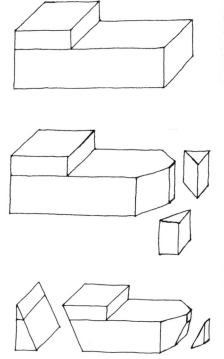

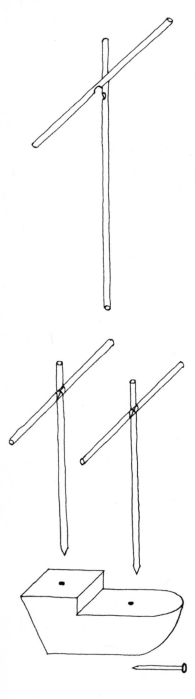

5. Saw the dowel rod into two 10 inch sections and two 8 inch sections. Cut a shallow notch in each 10 inch section, 1½ inches from one end. Cut a notch in the center of each 8 inch section. Place an 8 inch crossbar across each 10 inch mast, with the notches against each other. Tie the pieces of dowel rod tightly together with thread, and rub some glue on the thread. Wind more thread tightly around the dowel sections and rub on plenty of glue.

6. Paint a thin line around the nail, ½ inch from the point. Make a pencil mark exactly in the center of the rear deck, and another in the center of the front deck. Tap the nail lightly straight down on one of the pencil marks, until the painted line is even with the deck. Pull the nail out and do the same thing on the other pencil mark.

7. Use a knife or sandpaper to make a blunt point on the bottom of each mast. Put glue in the nail holes and push the masts into the holes. Before the glue dries, adjust the masts so that they stick straight up from the decks, with the crossbars going from side to side.

8. Push the nail straight into the bow, as far as the painted line, so that it sticks out in front of the ship. Pull it out, put glue

in the hole, and push the nail in again.

9. Paint the whole ship, except for the masts and crossbars, dark brown or black. Paint the decks tan or light brown. Use a light color and a very thin brush to paint on square gunport outlines along the sides of the ship.

10. Glue a sail to each of the crossbars. Tie a piece of thread from the head of the nail to the top of the front mast. Make the flag by folding the paper rectangle in half around the thread and gluing the two sides together. Paint the flag black, and then paint on a white skull-and-crossbones design.

School Projects

NATURAL RESOURCES MAP

On a sheet of oaktag draw an outline map of the United States or any other country you're studying in school. The map doesn't have to include every detail of the coastline or border, but the major features should be recognizable and in proportion to one another. If you are drawing the United States, for instance, Florida should be quite a lot bigger than Long Island, and Cape Cod should have a long, skinny, curving shape. After the outline is finished, draw in the lakes, rivers, and mountain ranges.

Make a list of the products of each state or region. An encyclopedia is very helpful for this. Cut out small balsa wood symbols to indicate each of the products—trees, corn cobs, cattle, fish, oil wells, and others. Glue each symbol to a little flat base, so that it stands up.

Glue the map down on a piece of masonite or thin plywood, cut to the right size. Then glue the balsa symbols in the appropriate spots on the map. Paint the name of the country at the top and paint on the names of the states, provinces, or regions. Then paint the balsa symbols in realistic colors—a corn cob, yellow, a cow, brown and white, and so on.

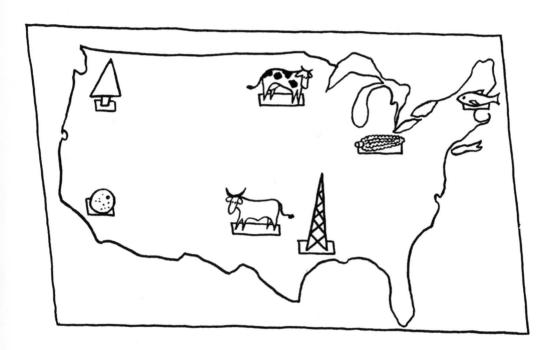

ANIMALS AROUND THE WORLD

If you're studying nature or conservation, you can use clothespin animals (see page 19) to make a school project. One idea is to make several of the animals native to a particular region. For the grasslands of Africa, for instance, you might make two lions, five or six zebras and antelopes, and a pair of giraffes. Baby animals, smaller ones like foxes, or short-legged ones like crocodiles are made by sawing off part of the clothespins to shorten the legs.

Use a large, shallow wooden box or the drawer from an old dresser or desk to display the animals as they would look in their natural surroundings. Fill the box with a layer of sand and stick in tufts of dry grass. Cut a small branch from a bush and put it in the sand at one corner of the box. Put the giraffes near it, as if they are feeding on the leaves of a tree. Arrange the other animals in little groups, with the lions creeping up through the thickest clumps of grass.

To show forest or jungle animals, you would fill the box with dark potting soil and use lots of cuttings taken from weeds and shrubs in a vacant lot.

A good conservation project can be made by showing different animals that are in danger of extinction. Mount the animals on a board with a label in front of each one, explaining why it is endangered and how it might be saved.

OTHER WAYS OF LIFE

In Social Studies you read about how people lived in the past and how they live in foreign countries today. You can learn about other ways of life and have fun at the same time when you make balsa models of different kinds of buildings. The ideas suggested here do not include step-by-step instructions. How you make your model will depend on what kind of project you have in mind. Several people in the class might each make a building of a different type. You can mount the models on a board, with a label identifying each one. Another approach would be to make a small village out of balsa wood, showing the way people live in one special area. To get more ideas, look at the pictures in an encyclopedia, or look at the dioramas and exhibits in a natural-history museum.

SOUTH AMERICAN STILT HOUSE—In some parts of South America, the people live in houses raised high in the air on wooden stilts. This protects them from the wet floor of the jungle, where rainfall is heavy and rivers often overflow their banks. The roofs are steeply slanted to shed the rain, and are thatched with overlapping layers of leaves. The walls are just open wooden frameworks because the jungle is very hot. The wind blowing through helps keep the houses cool.

It's easy to make this kind of house from thin strips of balsa. Just sand the strips to make them look like branches. After gluing the pieces together, tie them with pieces of thread.

NORTHWEST COAST INDIAN HOUSE—On the Pacific Coast of the United States and Canada, the Indians lived in buildings made of wide wooden boards. The houses had four corner posts and a roof framework made from the trunks of trees. The flat wall and roof boards were attached to the outside of the framework. There were no windows, but an oblong doorway was cut in one of the end walls. In front of each house stood a totem pole with carved bird and animal shapes. These shapes could be read as symbols telling the history of the owner's ancestors.

The framework and the totem pole might be made of balsa strips, ½ inch thick and ½ inch wide. Make the boards out of thin sheet balsa, cut in irregular widths. Balsa scraps form the wings and features of the totem pole figures.

MEDIEVAL CASTLE—The castle on page 22 illustrates life in Europe hundreds of years ago. Kings and noblemen made their homes in fortified stone castles and fought with each other for control of the land.

OTHER BUILDINGS YOU MIGHT WANT TO MAKE—Once you begin to think about the different kinds of buildings you can make, you'll discover that the possibilities are endless. Some ideas are an old-fashioned frontier fort, a Dutch windmill, an Oriental pagoda (temple), a Mexican hacienda (ranch house) with stables and a corral, and a Pueblo Indian village.

FAMOUS BUILDINGS

For a more complicated model-building project, you could make a copy of a famous building. You'll need to study photographs, make drawings, and plan your model carefully. Look in an encyclopedia or ask a librarian to help you find books with pictures of the building you plan to make. You don't have to show every single detail—if the shape and proportions are right, the model will look very impressive. When your building is finished, mount it on a base and prepare a short report on its history.

Some suggestions are the Alamo, the Empire State Building, the Eiffel Tower, and the United States Capitol Building (make the dome from half of a rubber ball).

Index

African-Lion Mask, 59-60
Angel Ornament, 37-38
Animals Around the World, 88-89
Armchair and Footstool, 47

Balancing Parrot, 18
Balsa Art, 51-62
Balsa Pendant, 64
Balsa Printing, 51-52
Balsa wood, buying, 9
Balsa wood, cutting, 14-15
Bookmarks, 63
Brushes, 11
Buckboard, Western, 77-79
Buildings, Famous, 94
Bullseye Box, 31-32

Castle, King Arthur's, 22-23
Chairs, *see* Doll Furniture
Christmas decorations, 36-38
Cleaning up, 17
Clothespin Zoo, 19-20
Coasters, 66
Cradle, 44
Cutting board, 10
Cutting tools, 9

Doll Furniture
    Cradle, 44
    Tables, 45-46
    Armchair and Footstool, 47
    Rocking Chair, 48-49
    Hammock, 50

Easter-Bunny Party Favor, 39

Famous Buildings, 94
Footstool, *see* Doll Furniture

Frog, Hopping, 26-28
Funny-Faces Mobile, 61-62
Furniture, *see* Doll Furniture

Games
    Bullseye Box, 31-32
    Jack-o-Lantern Marble Game, 43
    Shooting Gallery, 29-30
Gliders, balsa, 74
Gifts, 63-72
Glue, buying, 10
Glue, use of, 16

Hammock, 50
Hardware supplies, 11
Holiday and Party Fun, 33-43
Hopping frog, 26-28

Indian Shield, 55-56

Jack-o-Lantern Marble Game, 43

King Arthur's Castle, 22-23

Letter Holder, 67-68

Map, Natural Resources, 86-87
Mask, African-Lion, 59-60
Materials, *see* Tools and Materials
Medieval Castle, 93
Measuring and marking, 13
Midget Racer, 75-76
Mississippi Steamboats, 80-82
Mobile, Funny-Faces, 61-62
Models, 73-85

Natural Resources Map, 86-87
Northwest Coast Indian House, 92

Other Buildings You Might Want to
  Make, 94
Other Ways of Life, 90-93

Paint, buying, 10-11
Painting, 16-17
Parrot, Balancing, 8
Party Place Tags, 33-34
Pendant, Balsa, 64
Photograph Frame, 65
Pirate Ship, 83-85
Place Tags, Party, 33-34
Porch Chimes, 71-72
Potato Safari, 24-25
Printed Cards and Place Mats, 35
Printing, Balsa, 51-52

Racer, Midget, 75-76
Rocking Chair, 48-49

Salt and Pepper Server, 69-70
Sanding, 15-16
School projects, 86-94
School supplies, 11
Scraps, 11-12

Shield, Indian, 55-56
Ship, Pirate, 83-85
Shooting Gallery, 29-30
Star String, 36
Steamboat, Mississippi, 80-82
Stick Sculpture, 53-54.

Tables, *see* Doll Furniture
Tools and Materials, 9-12
Totem-Pole Wall Hanging, 57-58
Toys and Games, 18-32
Tracing, 13-14
Turkey Full of Nuts, 40-41

Valentine Plaque, 42

Western Buckboard, 77-79
Work area, preparation, 13
Working With Balsa Wood, 13-17

X-acto blades, 10
X-acto knife, 9

Zoo, Clothespin, 19-21